doll
Travel

Craft Your Way
Around the World

by **Emily Osborn**

★ American Girl®

Published by American Girl Publishing
Copyright © 2018 American Girl

Questions or comments? Call 1-800-845-0005,
visit **americangirl.com,** or write to Customer Service,
American Girl, 8400 Fairway Place, Middleton, WI 53562-0497.

Printed in China
18 19 20 21 22 23 QP 10 9 8 7 6 5 4 3 2 1

Editorial Development: Emily Osborn
Art Direction and Design: Dan Nordskog
Production: Jeannette Bailey, Kristi Lively, Cynthia Stiles
Photography: Joe Hinrichs, Youa Thao, Derrick Brabender
Craft Styling: Emily Osborn
Set Styling: Kim Sphar
Doll Styling: Kelly Erickson
Illustrations: Monika Roe

Photography & illustrations for kit supplies: Map—© iStock.com/RoyFWhlam (globe); © iStock.com/TomasSereda (Big Ben
& bridge); © iStock.com/franckreporter (Big Ben & sky); © iStock.com/Starcevic (Westminster Abbey); © iStock.com/andylid
(Tower Bridge); © iStock.com/fotoVoyager (Buckingham Palace). TV—© iStock.com/Grafner (coral reef). Camera—© iStock.com/
bluejayprints (zebras). Postcards— © iStock.com/pnphotos (Chinese New Year Parade); © iStock.com/Sisoje (Hindu temple); ©
iStock.com/IakovKalinin (Eiffel Tower); © iStock.com/GeorgeBurba (Hawaiian sunset); © iStock.com/ventdusud (Leaning Tower of
Pisa); © iStock.com/jejim (Venustiano Carranza Lighthouse); © iStock.com/narvikk (elephants); © iStock.com/johnkellerman (Big
Ben); © iStock.com/Tatiana_Ti (ohm).

Dear Doll Lover,

If you could go anywhere in the world, where would you go? Scuba diving on the Great Barrier Reef? Scooting around the streets of Italy? Going on safari in South Africa? You can imagine your ideal around-the-world vacation by creating doll-size trips using the ideas in this book. You'll also find a duffel bag, a passport, international maps, airline tickets, souvenirs, doll money, and more. It's everything you need to create a unique experience for your doll—and yourself.

Are you there yet?

Your friends at American Girl

Craft with Care

Keep Your Doll and Pet Safe

When creating doll or pet crafts, remember that dyes from ribbons, felt, beads, cords, fabrics, fleece, paint, and other supplies may bleed onto your doll and pet or their clothes and leave permanent stains. To help prevent this, use lighter colors when possible, and check your doll and her pet often to make sure the colors aren't transferring to their bodies, vinyl, or clothes or to the pet's fur. And never get your doll or pet wet! Water and heat greatly increase dye rub-off.

Get Help!

When you see this symbol 🖐★ in the book, it means that you need an adult to help you with all or a part of the craft. ALWAYS ask for help before continuing.

Ask First

If a craft asks you to use an old item, such as a shirt or sock, always ask an adult for permission before you use it. Your parent might still need it, so check first.

Craft Smart

If a craft instruction says "cut," use scissors. If it says "glue," use craft glue or adhesive dots. And if it says "paint," use a nontoxic acrylic paint. Before you use these supplies, ask an adult to check them over—especially paints and glues. Some crafting supplies are not safe for kids. Care should be taken when using battery-operated LED lights. They are not toys.

Put Up Crafts and Supplies

When you're not using the crafts or art supplies, put them up high or store them away from little kids and pets. Toddlers and animals might eat your crafts, break them, or even hurt themselves when playing with them.

WARNING
Safely tuck your doll away while you create crafts for her so that paint, glue, and other messy craft supplies don't get on your doll or her clothes. Make sure each project dries completely before using it near your doll.

Let's Get Ready!

Don't forget these items when traveling by land, air, or sea.

1. Travel Posters

Your doll is excited for an adventure! Put the **kit's travel posters** up on her wall for inspiration.

2. Travel Backpack

It is much easier to travel with a backpack than a heavy suitcase. To make one, attach two craft foam straps to the back of a fabric treat bag with adhesive dots. Slip the bag's cords through a wooden bead, and attach the cord with an adhesive dot. Fill the backpack with your doll's clothes and essential items for her trip, like the **kit's money and passport.** To decorate, use the **kit's travel stickers.**

3. Sleep Mask

Your doll can wear this to sleep on the plane. Trace the **kit's sleep mask pattern** onto a piece of fleece. Cut out the mask. Use adhesive dots to attach thick silk cord around the edges of the eye mask. Place adhesive hook-and-loop fasteners on each end to attach the sleep mask around your doll's head.

4. Toiletry Bag

Keep your doll's toiletries in their own separate bag. (Avoid liquids if she's flying!) ✋ Ask an adult if you can cut a rectangle from the corner of an old vinyl bag, keeping the zipper and zipper pull. Cover the zipper's cut with clear tape, and seal the two cut seams with adhesive dots.

5. Toiletries

Pack travel-size toiletries for the trip. Ask an adult if you can cut a square corner off an old washcloth. For a toothbrush, use adhesive dots to attach a white tube bead to a flattened piece of a drinking straw. For a bar of soap, glue together two white craft foam rectangles.

At the Airport

These items will make traveling more fun!

1. Duffel Bag

Fill the kit's duffel bag with your doll's clothes she might like for her trip. Don't forget to attach the kit's luggage tag so the bag doesn't get lost!

2. Travel Pillow

Pull out the kit's pillow pattern, and trace it twice on fleece. Cut out the pillow pieces, and glue the edges together, leaving one end open. Let dry. Stuff the pillow with fiberfill. Use an unsharpened pencil to push the filling all the way to the end, and then glue the opening closed. (If needed, use binder clips to hold the end until the glue dries.)

3. In-Flight Accessories

Fill your doll's backpack with any in-flight accessories she might like, such as the kit's deck of playing cards for a game of solitaire or the kit's map to study the streets of London before landing. And don't forget to pack some fun reading for her!

Hotel Room

These comforts can help a hotel feel like home.

1. End Tables

Wrap two empty plastic pint jars in washi tape. Paint the end tables with decoupage sealer to finish them and help the washi tape stick. Let dry. Place the **kit's tablet and cell phone** on the end tables so your doll can charge them.

2. Bolster

Wrap an 8-by-6-inch piece of fabric around a craft roll and tuck its ends into the roll's sides.

3. Television

Paint a 3½-inch wooden oval, a ½-by-¾-inch piece of thick craft foam, and a 3¼-by-5-inch piece of thick craft foam metallic black. Let dry. Glue the small piece of craft foam to the center bottom of the larger piece of craft foam. Let dry. Then glue the television to the center of the wooden oval for the base. Cut out a 3½-by-5¼-inch piece of black craft foam, and glue it to one side of the television. Place the **kit's television screen sticker** on the television for your doll to watch.

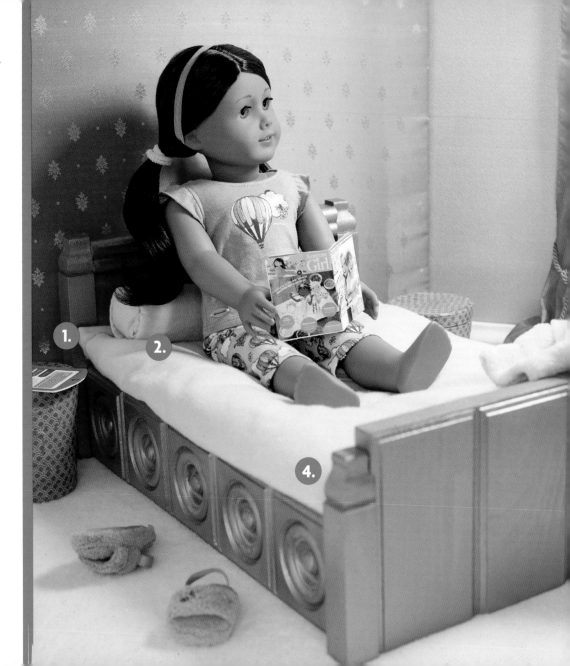

4. Bed You can find all the pieces for this comfy bed at your local hardware store.

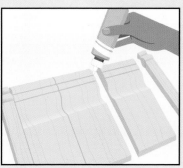

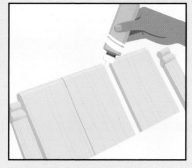

1. For the headboard, glue three 1-by-3½-by-7¾-inch Victorian plinth blocks together. Then glue one 1-by-1-by-8-inch hardwood inside corner piece to each side. Let dry.

2. For the footboard, glue three ⅞-by-3½-by-6-inch pine plinth blocks together. Then glue one 1-by-1-by-5½-inch hardwood inside corner piece to each side. Let dry.

3. For the frame, glue five ⅞-by-3½-inch square rosette moldings together. Let dry. Repeat for the other side.

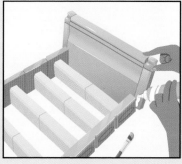

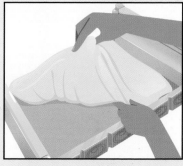

4. For the slats, glue together two ⅞-by-3½-by-5-inch plinth blocks. Let dry. Repeat four times. Glue the slats to the back of one frame piece. Let dry. Then glue the other end of the slat to the opposite frame piece. Make sure the two sides line up.

5. Paint the headboard, footboard, and frame a fun color, and let dry. Then glue the headboard to one end of the frame and the footboard to the other end. Let dry.

6. For a platform boxspring, ask an adult to help you cut out a 9½-by-19-inch piece of cardboard, and place it on top of the slats. For the mattress, fold a 19-by-38-inch piece of fabric in half.

Paris, France

Your doll will say "Oui-oui!" to picnicking along the Seine River.

1. Beret

🖐️ Trace the **kit's beret pattern** onto light-colored felt or wool. Cut out the pieces. Glue the pieces together (this is the inside of the hat). Let dry. Ask an adult to help you turn the hat right side out. Cut out a tiny piece for the top of the beret, and attach it with an adhesive dot.

2. Picnic Basket and Bread

Line a tiny basket with white tissue paper. Shape long, short, and round bread loaves from white, tan, or brown nontoxic clay. Use a butter knife or flat toothpick to make slits in the tops. Let dry. Brush the loaves with yellow, orange, red, and brown watercolor paint and let dry. Scrape a piece of white nontoxic sidewalk chalk with a craft stick to make some chalk powder, and sprinkle the chalk onto the bread for flour. Glue the bread into the basket.

3. Eiffel Tower

There are 5 billion lights on this tower, known as the "Iron Lady."

1. Paint two 8-inch wooden Vs and one 8-inch wooden I black. Let dry. Then glue the I to the bottom end of the two Vs. Let dry.

2. Trace the four sides of the tower onto black plastic mesh. Cut out and glue the mesh to each side of the tower. Let dry.

3. Cut out two 5-inch and two 4-inch pieces of cork for the big square, and two 3-inch and two 4-inch pieces for the little square. Paint the pieces black. Once they are dry, glue the matching pieces into squares. Let dry.

4. Slide the squares onto the tower from the top down, big square first. Paint a square toothpick black, and let dry; then use an adhesive dot to attach it to the top of the tower.

Cairns, Australia

Have a g'day exploring Down Under.

1. Great Barrier Reef

You should never get your doll wet, but you can create a play ocean by taping floral mesh over foam core and blowing bubbles. For the soft corals, use colorful craft moss, frilly scrunchies, and shower poufs. For the tube coral, use fabric curly bows. For sea anemones, use round sponges. For the hard coral, glue together colorful clothespins into fun shapes, and let dry. You can also use decorative balls for the hard, stony coral.

2. Scuba Gear

For the flippers, trace the kit's flipper pattern onto a piece of craft foam twice and cut them out. Ask a parent if you may glue or tape the flippers to a pair of doll shoes. Let dry. For the scuba mask, glue both ends of a 7-inch piece of elastic ribbon to a gum container lid. Place the mask around your doll's head to cover her eyes and nose. For the snorkel, place a marker cap on top of a reusable silicone straw. Tuck the straw into the side of the mask. For the oxygen tank, use a 7-by-2-inch (8-ounce) stainless steel spray bottle. Unscrew the spray tip from the spray head, and glue it to a marker cap. Glue the cap to the top of the bottle. Glue a 14-by-1-inch piece of elastic ribbon to the bottle. Wrap the ribbon around your doll's waist, and tape closed. Cut a 5-inch piece of black string, and tape it to the side of the bottle. For the mouthpiece, use a marker to color in one side of a ¾-inch wood wheel. Let dry. Attach this to the other end of the black string. Place an adhesive dot on the uncolored side, and attach it to your doll's mouth.

1. It's a Snap!
Capture your doll's memories with this handy digital camera.

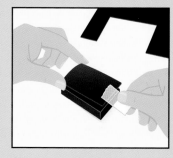

1. Paint a 1-by-2-inch **box lid** black. Let dry.

2. Trace the box lid on a piece of black **card stock**. Cut out the rectangle, and tape it to the back of the lid.

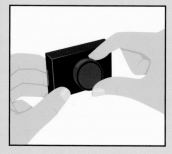

3. Tape a 1-inch black **plastic bottle cap** to the center of the box lid.

4. Place the **kit's camera stickers** onto the camera. Use adhesive dots to add a 9-inch **ribbon** for a strap.

Pisa, Italy
Scoot around this ancient site.

2. Leaning Tower of Pisa
Paint one 3-by-2-inch, one 3-by-3-inch, and five 3¾-by-2-inch round papier-mâché boxes ivory. Let dry. Stack them on a slight angle. Connect the boxes using adhesive dots.

3. Motor Scooter
To start, paint a 6-inch wooden L, a 6-by-3-inch piece of cork, and a 5-by-3-by-2½-inch wooden crate red. Let dry. For the seat, cover a 6-count egg carton in black fabric. Use duct tape to attach it to the bottom of the crate. Glue the long side of the L to the center of the cork; then glue the cork to the front end of the crate. Let dry. For the headlight, paint an old medicine cap red and yellow, and let dry. Glue it to the top of the L. For the body, trace the **kit's scooter pattern** onto red paper, and cut it out. Glue one end of the paper to the bottom of the cork and the other end to the front of the L, so the paper curves upward. Let dry.

Paint the bottom half of a mint tin silver. Let dry. For the wheels, wrap 2-inch-wide ribbon spools in black craft foam. Glue one wheel under the crate and the other to the inside of the mint tin. Glue the bottom of the mint tin to the front end. Paint two 3-inch paper straws, two ½-inch-wide buttons, two toothpicks, and two ½-inch pieces of toothpick silver. Let dry.

For the handlebars, wrap one end of each straw in washi tape. For the brake, glue the ½-inch piece of toothpick near the end of the straw. Glue to either side of the medicine cap. For mirrors, glue the buttons to the toothpicks; then glue the toothpicks to the medicine cap.

Place the **kit's Scoots sticker** on the front of the scooter and the **kit's license plate stickers** on the front and back bumpers.

3.

4.

Veracruz, Mexico

Traditional dance has deep roots in Mexican history and is used in celebrations today.

1. Sombrero

To make this traditional Mexican hat, trace a circle in the center of a round straw placemat using a 2½-by-3½-inch paper treat cup. Cut out the small circle, and then slip the treat cup through the hole. It should be a little snug. Roll the edges of the placemat to create a slight curl along the edges. Place the hat on your doll's head.

2. Poncho

Use a mini Christmas tree skirt as a poncho for your doll. Fold two sides of the tree skirt inward. Place the skirt around your doll's neck, close the poncho in the back with its hook-and-loop fasteners, and pull your doll's arms out the sides. Place adhesive dots on the skirt underneath the armholes to close the poncho on the sides.

3. Maracas

Sometimes called rumba shakers, these are used in pairs to create a nice percussive beat when shaken. To make play maracas, glue an oval-shaped bead to the end of a long bead. Let dry. Repeat for the second maraca.

4. Dress

Ask an adult if you can cut an old frilly skirt in half lengthwise. Cut small slits in either side, about 1 inch from the top, for armholes. Slip your doll's arms through the holes. Attach adhesive hook-and-loop fasteners to the back to close the dress around your doll.

19

KwaZula-Natal, South Africa

Go on safari to see beautiful animals in the wild.

1. Safari Hat

Protect your doll's face from the sun. Paint a doll-size wicker hat—found at craft stores—brown. Let dry completely before placing it on your doll's head.

2. Binoculars

Glue two medium-size fabric-marker caps to a small marker cap. Let dry. Use adhesive dots to attach a 9-inch-long piece of ribbon to each side of the binoculars so they can hang around your doll's neck.

3. White Rhinoceros

Roll two horns out of nontoxic air-dry white clay. Let dry. Use adhesive dots to attach one horn above your doll's pet's nose and the other on its nose.

4. Lion

Make a lion's mane for your doll's pet. Cut a 9-by-1-inch piece of fleece-lined fur. Wrap it around your pet's head, and secure it with an adhesive dot.

5. Elephant

For the ears, cut out two ovals from gray craft foam. Place an old hair elastic around your doll's pet's head. Use adhesive dots to attach the ears to either side of the elastic. For the trunk, cut a 4-by-5-inch piece of gray fabric. Use adhesive dots to attach it around an old hair elastic and to close the end of the fabric into the shape of an elephant trunk. For the tusks, use adhesive dots to attach 2 old glue caps to either side of the trunk. For the elephant's legs, cut out four 2-by-4-inch pieces of gray felt, and wrap them around the pet's legs. Use an adhesive dot to attach a small piece of gray felt to the pet's tail.

3.

Goa, India

Enjoy the colorful spices and captivating music of an Indian marketplace.

1. Marketplace

To create colorful **spice baskets,** wrap small bowls and baskets in vibrant cloth. For the spices, glue bright-colored pom-poms into the baskets. Hang up the **kit's prayer flags** with adhesive dots.

2. Bindi

Bindis have great religious significance in Hindu culture. Place the **kit's bindi** on your doll's forehead.

3. Sitar

For the body, paint a heart-shaped papier-mâché box, eight 1½-inch dowels, and six 1-inch wooden peg people shades of red. Paint a 2-by-1-inch wooden rectangle and a 1-inch wooden square silver. Let dry. Paint the edges of a heart-shaped spatula silver. Once dry, glue the box to the spatula. Glue the rectangle and square to the center of the spatula. Glue the eight dowels to the back of the handle. Let dry. Glue the six peg people to the top of the sitar. Once dry, attach a 12-inch piece of jeweled ribbon along the length of the sitar. Finally, glue a 1-inch wool or wood bead to the underside of the top of the handle.

4. Sari

The sari is the traditional outfit of Indian women.

1. Tuck one end of a cotton scarf into your doll's bottoms; then wrap it around your doll once, as shown.

2. Wrap the sari around once more, bringing the end up under your doll's right armpit.

3. Wrap the sari across the front, and tuck it into your doll's bottoms. Gather the loose end up and under your doll's left armpit.

4. Wrap the remaining fabric around your doll's back, underneath her right armpit and over her left shoulder. Ask an adult to pin the sari to her shirt if you like.

23

Beijing, China

Join the International Chinese New Year Parade celebration.

1. Qipao

During this celebration, wear new clothes, head-to-toe. Many opt to wear red, a very lucky color in Chinese culture. A *qipao* (pronounced chee-pow) is a one-piece dress. Cut a 12-by-16-inch piece of red or gold silky fabric. Cut two 1-inch slits for your doll's arms, 5 inches apart, about 1½ inches down from the top. Gently place your doll's arms through the holes. Tie a 14-inch piece of gold or red twisted cord around your doll's waist to secure the dress.

2. Dragon

Paint three craft rolls and two 5-inch wooden dowels yellow. Let dry. Use a piece of tape to attach the rolls. Cut fun shapes out of scrapbook paper for the eyes; then glue them onto either side of the dragon's head. Once dry, attach googly eyes. Use a black marker to draw the mouth. Use self-adhesive jewels for the nostrils. For fire, glue six 6-by-1-inch pieces of orange, yellow, and red tissue paper into the dragon's mouth. Finally, glue the two dowels to the bottom so your dolls can carry the dragon in the parade!

3. Celebrate!

Hang traditional red lanterns for a festive feel. Punch out the **kit's Chinese coins and red envelopes.** Place the money in the envelopes for your doll to give to her friends and family in honor of the new year.

1.

1. Cheese Girl Hat

These hats are traditionally worn by Dutch cheese girls in the marketplace.

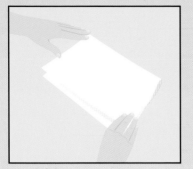

1. Fold an 8½-by-11-inch piece of white felt in half widthwise.

2. Fold the two top corners so that they meet in the middle.

3. Fold the bottom flap up (on the side facing away from you).

4. Fold the bottom flap up (on the side facing you).

5. Fold the corners down into little triangles.

6. Gently open the hat, and fold the ends up into little points. Place the hat on your doll's head.

Amsterdam, Netherlands

Explore the world of windmills and cheese in the "Venice of the North."

2. Windmill

Paint the top three inches of an 8-inch-diameter plastic planter white. Let dry. Paint a 5¾-inch-diameter papier-mâché box burnt orange. Let dry. Glue the papier-mâché box to the bottom of the plastic planter. Glue 4 unsharpened pencils together in an X shape. Let dry. For the sails, cut out four 6-by-2-inch pieces of white plastic mesh. Attach one sail to each pencil with adhesive dots. Attach a self-adhesive jewel to the center of the pencils; then glue the pencils to the top front of the windmill. For the door, cut out and attach a 3-by-2-inch piece of brown paper. Place paper grass stickers and the **kit's tulip stickers** around the bottom of the windmill for added detail.

3. Cheese

Roll yellow nontoxic air-dry clay into little balls; then gently flatten the sides to create cheese wheels. Let dry for at least 24 hours.

London, England
Cheers to a jolly time across the pond!

1. Telephone Booth

✋⭐ Ask an adult to help you cut a 17-by-6-inch rectangle from three sides of a 20-by-9-inch box. Paint the box red. Let dry. Paint four 18-by-¼-inch and twelve 7-by-¼-inch flat craft sticks red. Let dry. Use adhesive dots to attach two long flat craft sticks to one side of the phone booth. Then attach six of the smaller flat craft sticks, about 2 inches apart. Repeat for the other side. Use the **kit's phone booth template** to trace and cut four top pieces from red construction paper. Cut out a 9¼-inch square from red construction paper for the roof. Glue the four top pieces to the top of the booth. Once dry, glue the square piece to the top, pushing the corners down so the roof curves. Let dry. Use a glue stick or double-stick tape to attach the **kit's telephone and crown labels** to the phone booth. For the phone console, paint a 2½-inch papier-mâché box top silver. Let dry. For the phone, glue beads to either end of a 2-inch clothespin. For the cord, cut a hair tie in half. Glue one end of the hair tie to the bottom of the phone and the other to the bottom of the box top. Glue the top part of the phone to the center of the console. Let dry. Then glue the phone console inside the phone booth.

2. Royal Guard Bearskin Hat

Cut the bottom 6 inches off a furry bottle holder (found at your local craft store). Cut a 7-inch piece of gold cord or ribbon. Use adhesive dots to attach the ribbon to the inside of the hat. Place the hat on your doll's head.

2.

O'ahu, Hawai'i

Live *aloha* while taking in the beauty of the islands.

1. Accessories

Use adhesive dots to attach silk flowers or artificial leaves to one another to create flower crowns, leis, and grass anklets and wristlets.

2. Traditional Hula Outfit

For the skirt, cut the bottom end off a grass skirt (found at costume and party supply shops), making it 8 inches long to fit your doll. Wrap the skirt around your doll twice, and attach with its hook-and-loop fasteners. For the top, cut a 2-by-14-inch piece of fabric. Wrap the fabric around your doll, and knot it in the back.

3. Fire Stick

Wrap a 5-inch straw in washi tape. For the fire, attach orange, yellow, and red strips of tissue paper in either end using adhesive dots.

4. Pahu Drum

Cover a peanut butter jar in brown paper. Cover its lid in light brown craft foam. Cover the jar seam with washi tape. Use adhesive dots to attach white cord up and down the sides and artificial leaves around the top.

3.

Send it in!

What is your doll's favorite place to travel? To tell us, write to

Doll Travel **Editor**
American Girl
8400 Fairway Place
Middleton, WI 53562

(Sorry, but photos can't be returned. All comments and suggestions received by American Girl may be used without compensation or acknowledgment.)

Here are some other American Girl® books you might like:

Each sold separately. Find more books online at americangirl.com.

Parents, request a FREE catalog at **americangirl.com/catalog.**
Sign up at **americangirl.com/email** to receive the latest news and exclusive offers.

Discover online games, quizzes, activities,
and more at **americangirl.com**